P9-DBK-933

# *Jazz Chants*®
## *Old and New*

## CAROLYN GRAHAM

Marilyn Rosenthal
Developmental Editor

Oxford University Press

Oxford University Press
198 Madison Avenue
New York, NY 10016 USA
Great Clarendon Street
Oxford OX2 6DP England

*Oxford New York*
*Athens Auckland Bangkok Bogotá Buenos Aires Calcutta*
*Cape Town Chennai Dar es Salaam Delhi Florence Hong Kong Istanbul*
*Karachi Kuala Lumpur Madrid Melbourne Mexico City Mumbai*
*Nairobi Paris São Paolo Shanghai Singapore Taipei Tokyo Toronto Warsaw*

And associated companies in
*Berlin Ibadan*

OXFORD is a trademark of Oxford University Press.

ISBN 0-19-436694-4

Copyright © 2001 Oxford University Press

Library of Congress Cataloging-in-Publication Data

Graham, Carolyn.
  Jazz chants old and new / Carolyn Graham : Marilyn Rosenthal, developmental editor.
    p. cm.
  ISBN 0-19-436694-4
  1. English language--Textbooks for foreign speakers. 2. English language--Spoken
English--United States. 3. Jazz vocals--Texts. 4. Americanisms. 5. Readers. 6. Chants. I.
Rosenthal, Marilyn S., 1940-II. Title.
PE1128 .G6514 2001
  428.3'4--dc21                                                    00-044588

**No unauthorized photocopying.**

All rights reserved. No part of this publication may be reproduced, stored in a
retrieval system, or transmitted, in any form or by any means, electronic, mechanical,
photocopying, recording, or otherwise, without the prior written permission of Oxford
Universty Press.

This book is sold subject to the condition that it shall not, by way of trade or otherwise,
be lent, resold, hired out, or otherwise circulated without the publisher's prior consent in
any form of binding or cover other than that in which it is published and without a
similar condition including this condition being imposed on the subsequent purchaser.

Editorial Manager: Janet Aitchison
Senior Editor: Stephanie Karras
Developmental Editor: Marilyn Rosenthal, Syntactix International
Associate Production Editor: Justin Hartung
Design Manager: Lynne Torrey
Production Manger: Shanta Persaud

Printing (last digit): 10 9 8 7 6 5 4 3 2

Printed in Hong Kong

Cover design by Gail de Luca
Cover illustration by Neverne Covington
Handwriting by Don Grimes

"God Save the TOEFL Test," "Henry Wants to Go to Harvard," "I Told Him and He Told
Her," "The Telephone Rang, but I Didn't Answer It," "Cucamonga, California," "The
Chocolate Cake Song," and "Fresh Fish" reprinted with permisssion of Delta Systems Co., Inc.

"Tokyo Business Blues" reprinted with permission of Yohan Publishing Company.

# Acknowledgements

I wish to thank Stephanie Karras for her enthusiastic participation in this project and her tireless efforts to make this book a reality.

I would like to express my admiration and appreciation to Joey Mennonna for his brilliant work in arranging and performing the music on the accompanying cassette and compact disc.

Special thanks to the performers who joined me in recording the chants and songs: Rick Adamson, Todd Johnson, Jennifer Jay Myers, and Mona Stiles.

A special note of thanks and appreciation to my good friend, Marilyn Rosenthal, who was my guiding light and editor on the original *Jazz Chants* in 1978. It was my good fortune to have her brains and talent on this project as Developmental Editor for *Jazz Chants Old and New* in 2001.

Dedicated to Kid Ory, Jelly Roll Morton, Little M, and Keek

# Contents

# About Jazz Chants Old and New

## About this Book

The original *Jazz Chants* was first published in 1978. Since then, Carolyn Graham has written numerous other chants books for adults and children and has conducted jazz chants workshops throughout the world. In many of these workshops, she has found that the original *Jazz Chants* remains a favorite.

*Jazz Chants Old and New* offers the best of the classic *Jazz Chants* along with an exciting collection of new chants. A cassette or compact disc features performances of the chants set against a background of jazz music. In addition, Carolyn Graham has included a special section of songs, called Carolina Shout in Performance. These songs were written by Ms. Graham under her professional performance name of Carolina Shout. As Carolina Shout she performed piano concerts in the evening while teaching during the day at New York University and Harvard University.

The book is organized into seven parts:

Part I Classic Chants
Part II Classic Songs
Part III New Chants
Part IV New Songs
Part V Carolina Shout in Performance
Part VI Exercises for Chants and Songs
Part VII Answer Key

## What Is a Jazz Chant?

A jazz chant is the rhythmic expression of standard American English as it occurs in a situational context. The jazz chants included in this book and recorded on the accompanying cassette and CD are designed to reinforce the basic rhythm and intonation patterns of spoken American English. Just as a particular tempo and beat in jazz may convey powerful and varied emotions, the rhythm, stress, and intonation patterns of spoken American English are essential for the expression of feeling and intent. *Jazz Chants Old and New* sets authentic language to jazz rhythms. Linking these two dynamic forms has produced an innovative and effective approach to language learning.

Jazz chanting was developed primarily for the improvement of listening comprehension skills. The chants and songs included in this book reflect the authentic sounds of spoken American English, which often stretches, shortens, and drops sounds. These subtle features of the language are extremely difficult for students to understand unless their ear has been properly trained to understand the language of a native speaker in natural conversation. The question "Jeet yet?" is meaningless unless one has acquired the listening comprehension skills necessary to connect the sound with the words "Did you eat yet?" Other examples of blending sounds are I'm going to (gonna), I've got to (gotta), and I have to (hafta).

A comparison of the text of *Jazz Chants Old and New* and its cassette or compact disc helps to illustrate the striking difference between the written word and its spoken form. Jazz chants are particularly useful for developing these listening comprehension skills.

*Jazz Chants Old and New* also works well in reinforcing specific structures and vocabulary used in situational contexts. Many of the chants are written in two–part dialog form with extensive use of Yes/No Questions, Information Questions, Command and Response, and Exclamatory or provocative statements. The material in the chants is intended to provide the student with patterns and vocabulary that he or she can comfortably use in the world outside the classroom.

Throughout the world jazz chants have found an enthusiastic audience eager to practice the sounds and structures of conversational American English set to the powerful rhythms of American jazz. The rhythm is the glue that holds it together, and we find that the language "sticks" in our heads.

## Suggestions for Presenting the Chants and Songs

Jazz chants are based on model of repetition and learned response. The essential element in presenting a jazz chant is the clear, steady beat and rhythm.

### Step 1: Preview
Preview the chant with the class. Point out the title of the chant and ask students to predict what they think the chant is about. If necessary, explain the situational or cultural context of the chant.

### Step 2: Listen
Model the chant or play the recording to allow students to become familiar with the words and rhythm of the chant or the melody of the song. Encourage students to bring to class rhythmic instruments (tambourines, maracas, etc.) and play them in the rhythm of the chant as they listen. If students don't have rhythmic instruments suggest that they tap out the rhythm with a pencil or a ruler as they listen.

### Step 3: Choral Chanting
Have students repeat the lines of the chant following a model provided by the teacher and/or the recording. If students have particular difficulty with a word, a phrase, an idiom, or an expression, isolate it from the rest of the chant and have them practice with just that chunk of the language. It is often useful for students to practice the language of the chant with various small chunks before trying to chant, otherwise they could get lost in the written word and not concentrate on the natural rhythm and intonation of the spoken language.

### Step 4: Group/Individual Chanting
Once students are comfortable with the language and rhythm of the chant, divide the class into various groups to practice different stanzas of the chant or to practice the many question/response patterns in the chant. Encourage students to pantomime or act out the chant as they perform it.

After students have chanted in groups, have various pairs or individuals take turns chanting for the class.

### Extending and Reinforcing the Language of the Chants and Songs
Once students have practiced with the chants, an excellent way for them to internalize the language is to personalize it. Students can start simply, by substituting their names of individual words in various lines of the chant. For example, in the song, "Native Language," students could substitute personal information for the underlined words: He speaks Spanish. He was born in Lima.

Many of the chants lend themselves to role playing, which enables the students to move from the formal structure of the chants to an informal classroom improvisisation, using what they have learned in a situational context. These improvisations give students not only the opportunity to speak individually but to make choices of attitudes in their responses. During the role playing, it is important to make sure that students retain the rhythm and intonation patterns established earlier.

## The Exercises

The exercises for the chants and songs begin on page 67. Use the Answer Key on pages 96–100 as your script for the dictation and cloze exercises.

# Structure Key

## Present Continuous

## Pronouns: subject/object

## Questions: *Wh-* questions

## Questions: Yes/No questions

## Two-Word Verbs

## Verb + Infinitive

# Part I

## Classic Chants

✦ This chant illustrates several ways to complain about noise, from the gentle *Sh!* and *Please be quiet!* to the stronger *Keep it down!* and *Stop that noise!*

✦ **Sh! Sh! Baby's Sleeping!** provides practice in the present continuous *is sleeping* in contrast to the simple past *What did you say?/I said.*

✦ Have students listen for and practice the pronunciation of:

— the contraction of *Baby is* in *Baby's sleeping;*

— the final *-ing* sound in *sleeping;*

— the reduction of *did you* to *didja* in *What did you say?*

✦ Introduce the chant by asking students what they usually say when someone is making too much noise. Write their answers on the board, including the expressions from the chant: *Sh, Please be quiet, Keep it down, Stop that noise.*

# 1 Sh! Sh! Baby's Sleeping!

I said, "Sh! Sh! Baby's sleeping!"
I said, "Sh! Sh! Baby's sleeping!"

    What did you say?
    What did you say?

I said, "Please be quiet! Baby's sleeping!"
I said, "Please be quiet! Baby's sleeping!"

    What did you say?
    What did you say?

I said, "Keep it down! Baby's sleeping!"
I said, "Keep it down! Baby's sleeping!"

    What did you say?
    What did you say?

I said, "Stop that noise! Baby's sleeping!"
I said, "Stop that noise! Baby's sleeping!"

WAAAAAAAAAAAAAAA!

Not anymore!

✦ This chant provides practice in the simple present question *Do you know…?* and the emphatic short response *Yes, of course I do.*

✦ Call students' attention to the rising Yes/No question intonation in *Do you know Mary?* and *Do you know her little brother?* versus the falling Wh- question intonation pattern of *Mary who?* Also, point out that the *h* sound in *her* is dropped when we say *know her* and *and her.*

✦ **Do You Know Mary?** may be used for practice in negative short answers plus follow-up questions in question-response combinations such as *Do you know Mary? No, I don't. Do you?* Have students listen for and practice the rising intonation of the follow-up questions.

✦ Once students are familiar with the chant, have them practice it, substituting their own names and the names of their family members.

# 2 Do You Know Mary?

Do you know Mary?
 Mary who?
Mary McDonald.
 Of course I do.

Do you know her little brother?
 Yes, of course I do.
 I know her brother
 and her mother
 and her father, too.

Do you know her older sister?
 Yes, of course I do.
 I know her older sister, Betty,
 and her younger sister, Sue.

Do you know her Aunt Esther?
 Yes, of course I do.
 I know her aunts and her uncles
 and her cousins, too.

Do you know her husband, Bobby?
 Yes, of course I do.
 I know her husband and his brother
 and his father, too.

✦ This chant is particularly effective if one begins with a rather slow beat, starting very softly, and gently building the sound until it evokes an image of the giant redwood trees of California. Point out the long, stretched-out sound of *tall trees* versus the thick, shorter sound of *big*.

✦ Another way to perform **Tall Trees** is to begin with an opening chorus of voices that continues in unison, providing a steady beat and background for a soloist. Assign the solo voice either to one student or to a group of students speaking in unison. The soloist enters with *The coast of California is a beautiful sight*, keeping within the beat and rhythm of the chorus, which continues to chant while the soloist speaks. Have students repeat the entire chant at least three times, increasing the volume each time and ending with a very full sound for *Big trees, tall trees./ Big, tall trees.*

# 3 Tall Trees

### *SOLO*

Tall trees.
Tall trees.
Big, tall trees.

Tall trees.
Tall trees.
Big, tall trees.

### *CHORUS*

Tall trees, tall trees.
Big, tall trees.
Tall trees, tall trees.
Big, tall trees.

Tall trees, tall trees.
Big, tall trees.
Tall trees, tall trees.
Big, tall trees.

Big trees, tall trees.
Big trees, tall trees.
Big trees, tall trees.
Big, tall trees.

### *SOLO*

The coast of California
is a beautiful sight,
with the tall trees, tall trees.
Big, tall trees.

The coast of California
is a beautiful sight,
with the tall trees, tall trees.
Big, tall trees.

✦ This chant illustrates the use of the past continuous *It was raining* with the simple past *I got wet/I stayed outside*. Point out how the past continuous is used to describe background, while the simple past introduces action.

✦ Have students listen for and practice the *-ing* sound in *raining, falling, soaking*.

✦ The presentation of **Rain** should echo the sound of a light spring rain, with the volume and speed increasing until it sounds like a downpour. The mood can then be changed by decreasing the speed and volume, until there is just the sound of a few raindrops and finally silence. The last four lines of the chant can be presented with both voices speaking together simultaneously.

# 4 Rain

It was raining, raining, raining hard.
It was falling on my head.
    It was falling on the stars.
It was falling on the sun.
    It was falling on my shoes.
I got soaking wet.
    I got soaking wet.
But I stayed outside.
    I stayed outside.
The rain was sweet.
    The rain was warm.
The rain was soft.
It reminded me of home.

It was raining, raining, raining hard.
    It was falling, falling, falling on the stars.

Soft rain.
    Raining, raining.
Sweet rain.
    Raining, raining.
Warm rain.
    Raining, raining.

| *SOLO* | *CHORUS* |
|---|---|
| Sweet, soft, | Raining, raining. |
| warm rain. | Raining, raining. |
| Sweet, soft, | Raining, raining. |
| warm rain. | Raining, raining. |

✦ This chant provides practice in the question pattern *How do you like…?* in reference to the preparation of food and beverages. Point out the difference in meaning between the questions *How do you like your eggs?* (asking the person to make a choice: *boiled, fried*, etc.) and *How do you like your job?* (asking for an opinion: *I love it, I can't stand it*, etc.).

✦ Have students listen for and practice the pronunciation of:

— the *z* sound of the plural *s* in *eggs*;

— the final *d* sound in *scrambled* and *boiled* versus the final *t* sound in *poached*.

✦ Point out the use of the noncommittal answer *I don't care*, which returns the choice to the person asking the question. Encourage students to practice with other similar expressions, such as *It doesn't make any difference to me, It doesn't matter, It's all the same to me.*

# 5 Major Decisions

How do you like your coffee?
> Black. Black.

How do you like your tea?
> With lemon, please.

How do you like your steak?
> Medium rare.

How do you like your eggs?
> I don't care.

Sunny-side up?
> I don't care.

Poached on toast?
> I don't care.

Scrambled, with bacon?
> I don't care.

Over-easy?
> I don't care.

Soft-boiled? Hard-boiled?
> I don't care.

How about an omelet?
> I don't care.

Come on, tell me.
This isn't fair!
> I told you the truth.
> I really don't care!

# 6 Banker's Wife's Blues

**NOTES**

✦ This chant provides practice in *Wh-* questions with *Where, When,* and *Why* in the simple present, and corresponding responses—focusing on third-person singular forms.

✦ Have students listen for and practice:

— the falling intonation of information questions with *Where, When,* and *Why;*

— the pronunciation of the *z* sound of the third-person singular endings in *lives, loves,* and *studies;*

— the pronunciation of the *s* sound of the third-person singular ending in *works* and *sleeps.*

Where does he live?
> He lives near the bank.

Where does he work?
> He works at the bank.

When does he work?
> He works all day
> and he works all night
> at the bank, at the bank,
> at the great big bank.

Where does he study?
> He studies at the bank.

Where does he sleep?
> He sleeps at the bank.

Why does he spend all day, all night,
all day, all night
at the bank, at the bank,
at the great big bank?
> Because he loves his bank
> more than his wife,
> and he loves his money
> more than his life.

✦ This chant provides practice
in giving an appropriate
response or suggestion to a
complaint. It uses the simple
present to indicate a condition
*(My feet hurt!)* and the command
response to indicate an
appropriate action or
suggestion *(Take off your shoes.)*.
**My Feet Hurt!** also provides
practice with the two-word
verbs *take off* and *put on* as well
as the expressions *It's hot/It's
cold* to talk about temperature.

✦ Have students listen for and
practice the *z* sound of plural *s*
in *hands, gloves,* and *shoes.*

# 7 My Feet Hurt!

My feet hurt!
 Take off your shoes.
My feet hurt!
 Take off your shoes.
My feet hurt!
 Take off your shoes.
My feet hurt!
 Take off your shoes.
It's hot in here!
 Take off your sweater.
It's hot in here!
 Take off your sweater.
It's hot in here!
 Take off your sweater.
My feet hurt!
 Take off your shoes.

It's cold in here!
 Put on your sweater.
It's cold in here!
 Put on your sweater.
It's cold in here!
 Put on your sweater.
My feet hurt!
 Take off your shoes.

My hands are cold!
 Put on your gloves.
My hands are cold!
 Put on your gloves.
My hands are cold!
 Put on your gloves.
My feet hurt!
 Take off your shoes.

# 8 Departure and Return Home

**NOTES**

✦ This chant provides practice in affirmative and negative command forms and the *I will/I won't* responses to those commands. Point out that *will* is used in response to affirmative commands (*Don't worry, I will.*) and *won't* is used in response to negative commands (*Don't worry, I won't.*).

✦ Have students listen for and practice the pronunciation of:

— the contractions *don't, won't, it's,* and *I'm;*

— the final *t* sound in the past form *missed.*

**Departure**

Have a wonderful trip!
Have a wonderful trip!
Don't forget to call me
when you get back.

    Have a wonderful trip!
    Have a wonderful trip!
    Don't forget to call me
    when you get back.

Have a wonderful trip!
    Don't worry, I will.
Have a wonderful trip!
    Don't worry, I will.
Don't forget to call me.
    Don't worry, I won't.
Don't forget to call me.
    Don't worry, I won't.

**Return Home**

Gee, it's good to see you.
You look wonderful.
    So do you.
It's been a long time.
    It sure has.
It's been a long time.
    It sure has.
I missed you terribly.
    Me too.
I'm so glad you're back.
    So am I.

✦ This chant provides practice using *Wh-* questions with *What* (*What time is it?*). It also illustrates the use of command forms with and without the additional polite word *please*.

✦ Have students listen for and practice the pronunciation of:

— the informal spoken form of *going to: gonna*;

— the contractions *we're, I'm,* and *don't*.

✦ The presentation of **Panic on Being Late** could reflect a sense of growing panic by starting slowly and softly and then increasing the speed and volume as the chant progresses. This same approach can be used with different repetitions of the entire chant.

# 9 Panic on Being Late

What time is it?
What time is it?
    Hurry up! Hurry up!
    Hurry up! Hurry up!

What time is it?
What time is it?
    Please hurry up!
    We're going to be late.

Oh, I don't have time
to talk to you now.
I'm late, I'm late, I'm terribly late.
    Hurry up! Hurry up!
What time is it?
    Hurry up! Hurry up!
What time is it?
    Hurry up!
What time is it?
    Hurry up!

## NOTES

✦ This chant provides practice in *Wh-* questions with *Where, How, How much,* and *Why,* as well as in Yes/No questions. Point out the difference between the falling intonation pattern of *Wh-* questions *(Where were you last night?)* and the rising intonation pattern of Yes/No questions *(Did you have a good time?)*.

✦ Explain that the first two questions in the chant are perfectly acceptable *(Where are you from?* and *Where were you born?)*. The questions then become increasingly personal, asking for information that would be considered private in the United States. Questions such as these would be viewed as rude by most people in the U.S. unless asked by very close friends or relatives. The response *I'd rather not say* provides a polite way of avoiding answering inappropriate questions.

Where were you born?
    I'd rather not say.

Where are you from?
    I'd rather not say.

How tall are you?
How old are you?
How much do you weigh?
    I'd rather not say.

How much rent do you pay?
    I'd rather not say.

How much do you make?
    I'd rather not say.

Why aren't you married?
    I'd rather not say.

Why don't you have children?
    I'd rather not say.

Where were you last night?
Why weren't you home?
Did you stay out late?
Did you come home alone?
Did you have a good time?
Did you see a good play?
Did you go to a concert?
    I'd rather not say.

✦ This chant provides practice in the use of the modal auxiliaries *shouldn't* and *ought to* for giving advice and making suggestions.

✦ **Mama Knows Best** also offers practice with the demonstrative adjectives *this* and *that*.

✦ Have students listen for and practice the conversational pronunciation of *ought to: oughta.*

# 11 Mama Knows Best

You shouldn't do it that way.
You ought to do it this way.
>You ought to do it this way.
>You ought to do it my way.

You shouldn't wear it that way.
You ought to wear it this way.
>You ought to wear it this way.
>You ought to wear it my way.

You shouldn't go with them.
>You ought to go with us.
You shouldn't take the train.
>You ought to take the bus.

You shouldn't wear that earring.
>You ought to cut your hair.
You shouldn't eat that junk food.
>You ought to eat a pear.

You shouldn't do it that way.
>You ought to do it this way.
>You ought to do it this way.
You ought to do it my way.

# 12 On the Rocks

◆ This chant provides practice in the simple present with an emphasis on the third-person singular. Point out the use of the frequency adverb *never* as in *He never listens to me,* and contrast this with the negative statement *He doesn't listen to me.*

◆ Have students listen for and practice the three different pronunciations of the simple present third-person singular endings:

— the *z* sound in *listens*;

— the *s* sound in *talks* and *sits*;

— the *iz* sound in *watches*.

You never listen to me.
What did you say?
You never listen to me.
What?

He never listens to me.
He never talks to me.
He just sits around
and watches TV.

She never listens to me.
She never talks to me.
She just sits around
and watches TV.

She never listens to me.
She just sits around.
She never talks to me.
She just sits around.
She just sits around.
She just sits around
and watches TV.
She just sits around.

He never listens to me.
He just sits around.
He never talks to me.
He just sits around.
He just sits around.
He just sits around
and watches TV.
He just sits around.

✦ This chant provides practice in the possessive pronouns *mine, his,* and *yours.* Have students listen for and practice the final *z* sound in *his* and *yours.*

✦ **Taking Credit** also offers practice with negative statements and questions with *not,* the contractions *it's* and *I'm,* and the use of *certainly* and *of course* for emphasis.

✦ This chant provides practice in various types of intonation patterns. Point out the rising intonation of Yes/No questions and the falling intonation of *Wh-* questions. Call attention to the way the question *It's his?* is transformed into an exclamation through intonation alone: *It's his!* Have students listen for and practice the rising Yes/No question intonation of *It's his?* versus the rising-falling statement or exclamation intonation of *It's his!*

# 13 Taking Credit

Whose book is this?
    It's mine!
    It's mine!
Are you sure it's not his?
    No, no, it's mine!

Whose work is this?
This beautiful work!
    It's mine! It's mine!
    It's mine! It's mine!

Whose work is this?
This awful work!
    It's his! It's his!
    It's his! It's his!

Are you sure it's not yours?
    Of course it's not mine!
    It's certainly not mine!
    Not mine, not mine!

Not yours?
    Not mine!
Are you sure?
    I'm sure!
It's his?
    It's his!
Not yours?
    Not mine!

# 14 It's Got to Be Somewhere

+ This chant offers practice with the commands *Take it easy, Try to remember*, and *Think back* as helpful suggestions to someone who is upset over having lost or misplaced something. It also practices the idiomatic expression *Thank heavens* to express thankfulness about good news and the exclamation *Whew!* to express relief.

+ The chant also provides practice in the use of the modals *have got to, have to,* and *must* to express different degrees of certainty. Point out the contraction *It's* in *It's got to be here!* and in *It's gone!* Explain that in the first example, the *'s* stands for *has (It has)*; in the second, the *'s* stands for *is (It is)*.

+ Notice that the pronoun *she* in the fourth and second-from-last lines of the chant refers to the first speaker. *She* should be changed to *he* if the first speaker is a male.

Where is it? Where is it?
> Where is it? Where is it?

I can't find it.
> She can't find it.

It's got to be here. It's got to be here.
> It has to be here. It must be here.

It's gone! It's gone!

It's gone! It's gone!
> Take it easy! Take it easy!

It has to be here.

It must be here.
> It can't be lost.
> It can't be lost.

It's got to be here.

It's got to be here.
> Try to remember.
> Try to remember.

I can't remember.
> Try to remember.

I can't remember.
> Think back.

I can't think.
> Think back.

I can't think.
> Where did you put it?
> Where did you put it?

I can't remember.

I can't remember.

Oh! Here it is! Here it is!

Thank heavens!
> Thank heavens!

I found it.
> She found it.

Here it is! Here it is!
> Whew!

✦ This chant provides practice in the type of question that calls for repetition or confirmation of information. These questions have a rising intonation in the chant even when they are *Wh-* questions in form. Have students listen for and practice these rising-intonation questions asking for repetition of information: *How many cans? Did you say twelve? Twelve cans of fish?*

✦ The chant also provides practice with the quantity expressions *a lot of* and *too much*. Also point out the emphatic short response *It sure is!*

✦ **Twelve Cans of Tuna Fish Rag** provides practice in the falling intonation pattern commonly used for *Wh-* questions, as in *What kind of fish?* and *How often does she eat those twelve cans of tuna?*

✦ The chant should be presented in a quick, bright manner, similar to the sounds of early American ragtime music.

# 15 Twelve Cans of Tuna Fish Rag

Twelve cans. Twelve cans.
Twelve cans of tuna fish.
Twelve cans.
    How many cans?
Twelve, twelve.
    Did you say twelve?
Yes, I said twelve.
    Twelve cans of what?
Twelve cans of fish.
    Twelve cans of fish?
Yes, fish. Yes, fish.
    What kind of fish?
Tuna, tuna.
    Twelve cans of tuna fish?
Yes, twelve cans.
    How often does she eat
    those twelve cans of tuna?
    How often does she eat
    those twelve big cans?
Every night. Every night.
She eats twelve cans of tuna fish
every night.
    Twelve cans of tuna fish
    every night?
    Twelve cans? That can't be right!
That's a lot of tuna.
    It sure is!
That's a lot of tuna.
    It sure is!
That's too much tuna, if you ask me.
    It sure is! It sure is!
Twelve cans of tuna is a lot of fish,
if you ask me, if you ask me.
    It sure is!
    It sure is!

✦ This chant provides practice in forming past tense *Wh-*questions with *What* and *Why.* Point out that negative *Wh-*questions such as *Why didn't you sell it?* and *Why didn't you give it to him?* usually express an attitude of surprise or anger on the part of the speaker. As with all *Wh-* questions, however, they ask for information and have a falling intonation.

✦ Other questions in this chant confirm or ask for information, and have a rising intonation. Have students listen for and practice these rising-intonation questions: *What did you say? You what? Gave it away? Sell it?*

✦ **I Gave It Away** offers practice in the object pronouns *me, him, her,* and *them.*

# 16  I Gave It Away

I gave it away.
> You what?

I gave it away.
> What did you say?

I said, "I gave it away."
> Gave it away?

That's what I said.

I said, "I gave it away."
> Why?

Because I wanted to.
> You wanted to?

Yes, I wanted to.
> Why didn't you sell it?

Sell it?
> Yes, sell it. Sell it.
> Why didn't you sell it?

I didn't want to.
> Why not? Why not?

I didn't want to.
> Why not? Why not?

I didn't want to.
> Why didn't you give it to me?

I didn't want to.
> Why didn't you give it to him?

I didn't want to.
> Why didn't you give it to her?

I didn't want to.
> Why didn't you give it to them?

I didn't want to.

I didn't want to.

✦ This chant provides practice in the possessive pronouns *mine, yours, his, hers, ours,* and *theirs,* and in the demonstrative pronouns *this* and *that.* The chant also illustrates the use of the present continuous *What are you doing with that?* to indicate immediate action taking place.

✦ Have students listen for and practice the conversational reduction of *What are you doing...?* to *Whaddaya doing...?*

# 17 Selfish

This is mine.
That's yours.
Don't touch mine.
Get your own.

    This is mine.
    That's yours.

This is mine.
That's yours.

    This is mine.
    That's yours.
    That's yours.
    That's yours.

Hey, what are you doing?
What are you doing with that?
That's mine.

    Hey, what are you doing?
    What are you doing with that?
    That's his.

Hey, what are you doing?
What are you doing with that?
That's hers.

    What's mine is mine.
    What's yours is yours.

What's his is his.
What's hers is hers.

    What's ours is ours.
    What's theirs is theirs.

# 18 Easy Solutions

Gee, I'm hungry.

    Have a sandwich.

Gee, I'm angry.

    Calm down.

Gee, I'm sleepy.

    Take a nap.

Gee, it's chilly in here.

    Put on a sweater.

Gee, it's hot in here.

    Open a window.

I've got the hiccups.

    Drink some water.

My nose itches.

    Scratch it.

My feet hurt.

    Sit down for awhile.

My shoes are tight.

    Take them off.

I have a toothache.

    Go to the dentist.

I have a headache.

    Take some aspirin.

I'm lonely.

    Call up a friend.

I'm bored.

    Go to a movie.

# 19 Wake Up! Wake Up!

✦ This chant provides practice in the command forms *Wake up, Get up*, and in the use of the expression *Come on* for encouragement or pleading. It also illustrates the use of the modals *have to, must*, and *have got to* to express obligation.

✦ **Wake Up! Wake Up!** also provides practice in the future with *be going to (You're going to be late!)* and *want* followed by the infinitive of another verb (*I don't want to get up.*).

✦ Have students listen for and practice the conversational reductions in the following sentences:

— *You've got to*    = *You've gotta*
    *get up.*            *get up.*

— *I don't want to* = *I don't wanna*
    *get up.*            *get up.*

— *You're going to* = *You're gonna*
    *be late.*            *be late.*

Wake up! Wake up!
    What time is it?
Wake up! Wake up!
    What time is it?
It's time to get up.
    What time is it?
It's time to get up.
    What time is it?
Come on, get up!
    I don't want to get up.
Come on, get up!
    I don't want to get up.
You have to get up!
    I don't want to get up.
You must get up!
    I don't want to get up.
You've got to get up!
    I don't want to get up.
Come on, get up!
    I don't want to get up.
Get up! Get up!
You're going to be late!
    Late for what?
Late for work.
    Late for work?
    It's Sunday!

✦ This chant provides practice in affirmative and negative short response forms, moving from *be* to other verbs: *Yes, you are/No, I'm not. Yes, she does/No, she doesn't.*

✦ Have students listen for and practice the sharp contrast in rhythm and stress between *Yes, you are/No, I'm not* and the more emphatic *You are too/I am not.*

# 20 You're Just Like Your Mother

Stop it!
    Stop what?
Stop arguing with me.
    I'm not arguing with you.
Yes, you are.
    No, I'm not.
Yes, you are.
    No, I'm not.
You are too!
    I am not!
You are too!
    I am not!
You're just like your mother.
    I am not!
Yes, you are!
    No, I'm not!
Yes, you are!
    No, I'm not!
She loves to argue.
    No, she doesn't!
Yes, she does!
    No, she doesn't!
Yes, she does!
    No, she doesn't!
She does too!
    She does not!
She does too!
    She does not!
Don't argue with me!

# Part II

## Classic Songs

# 21 Native Language

◆ This song provides practice in simple present third-person singular forms. Have students listen for and practice the *s* sound of the third-person marker in the verb *speaks*.

◆ **Native Language** also provides practice in the simple past form of the irregular verb *grow up (grew up)* and in the expression *was born*. Point out the use of *in* in the prepositional phrases *in Boston, in Lima,* and *in Moscow*.

Melody: "Frere Jacques"

He speaks English.
He speaks English.
So does she.
So does she.
He was born in Boston.
He grew up in Boston.
So did she.
So did she.

He speaks Spanish.
He speaks Spanish.
So does she.
So does she.
He was born in Lima.
He grew up in Lima.
So did she.
So did she.

He speaks Russian.
He speaks Russian.
So does she.
So does she.
He was born in Moscow.
He grew up in Moscow.
So did she.
So did she.

# 22 God Save the TOEFL Test

✦ This song provides practice in the simple past form of the irregular verbs *take, think, be, get,* and *become (took, thought, was, got, became)* and in the simple past regular verb forms *tried, filled, wasted, promised.*

✦ Have students listen for and practice the three sounds of the regular past *ed* endings, such as:

— the *d* sound in *filled;*

— the *id* sound in *wasted;*

— the *t* sound in *promised.*

✦ Also have students listen for and practice the *z* sound of the plural *s* in *eyes, tears,* and *years.*

✦ Point out and have students practice the rhyming words in the song: *test/best, take/stomachache/break, tears/years, promised me/ fluently/became of me.*

Melody: "God Save the Queen"

I took the TOEFL test.
I thought I did my best.
I really tried.

That test was hard to take.
I got a stomachache.
I thought my heart would break
at the TOEFL test.

My eyes filled up with tears.
I wasted all those years
on English class.

My teacher promised me
that I'd speak fluently.
I don't know what became of me
at the TOEFL test.

# 23 Henry Wants to Go to Harvard

✦ This song provides practice in the use of the verb *want* followed by the infinitive form of another verb: *wants to graduate, wants to learn, wants to go, wants to reach, wants to be,* and *doesn't want to drive.*

✦ Point out the pronunciation of the third-person *s* in the affirmative form *he wants* versus the base form *want* in the negative *he doesn't want.*

✦ Have students practice the pronunciation of the indefinite articles used in the song: *an MBA, an inexpensive car, a star, a cell phone, a VCR.* Also point out and have students practice the song's rhyming words: *fail/Yale/sail, star/car/VCR.*

Melody: "The Battle Hymn of the Republic"

Henry wants an MBA.
He doesn't want to fail.
Henry wants to graduate
from Harvard or from Yale.
Henry wants to learn to ski.
He wants to learn to sail,
but Henry wants an MBA
from Harvard.

Henry wants to go to Harvard.
Henry wants to go to Harvard.
Henry wants to go to Harvard,
'cause Henry wants an MBA.

Henry wants to reach the top.
He wants to be a star.
Henry doesn't want to drive
an inexpensive car.
Henry has a cell phone.
Henry has a VCR,
but Henry wants an MBA
from Harvard.

Henry wants to go to Harvard.
Henry wants to go to Harvard.
Henry wants to go to Harvard,
'cause Henry wants an MBA
from Harvard.
Henry wants an MBA.

**Note:** This song was created and perfomed at Harvard University Press with my friends and colleagues Barbara Levy, Eric Dwyer, and Deryn Verity

# 24 Love Song

✦ This song provides practice in forming Yes/No questions in the simple present with *be* and other verbs. It also provides practice with Yes/No questions using the future with *will*. Have students listen for and practice the contrasting question and short-answer pattern with *be*, *does*, and *will*. For example:

*Is she happy?*      *Yes, she is.*

*Does she love him?*      *Yes, she does.*

*Will she hug him?*      *Yes, she will.*

✦ Point out that pronouns such as *he, him, her* usually lose the initial *h* sound except when they begin a sentence. Have students listen for and practice the following phrases: *Does he, is he, will he, hug her, kiss her, leave her, hug him, kiss him, leave him, love her, love him.*

✦ Have students practice the rising intonation pattern in the Yes/No questions throughout the song.

✦ Call attention to the vowel sounds in *love* versus *leave* and to the *z* sound of the third-person marker in *knows.*

Melody: Traditional American Hymn

Does she love him?

    Yes, she does.

Is she happy?

    Yes, she is.

Does he know it?

    Yes, he does. Yes, he knows it.

Will she hug him?

    Yes, she will.

Will she kiss him?

    Yes, she will.

Will she leave him?

    Yes, she will, if she has to.

Does he love her?

    Yes, he does.

Is he happy?

    Yes, he is.

Does she know it?

    Yes, she does. Yes, she knows it.

Will he hug her?

    Yes, he will.

Will he kiss her?

    Yes, he will.

Will he leave her?

    Yes, he will, if he has to.

Are they happy?

    Yes, they are.

Are they lucky?

    Yes, they are.

Do they know it?

    Yes, they do. Yes, they know it.

Will he find somebody new?

Will she find somebody, too?

    Yes, they will.

    Yes, they will, if they have to.

# 25 I Told Him and He Told Her

## NOTES

✦ This song provides practice in the simple past form of the irregular verb *tell (told)* as well as in the use of the subject pronouns *I, he,* and *you,* and the object pronouns *him, her,* and *you.* Point out the use of *who* as a subject in *Who told you?* and of *everybody* with the third-person singular form *knows.*

✦ Point out that the falling intonation pattern of the *Wh-* question *Who told you?* is the same as that of statements such as *I told him* and *I told her.*

Melody: "Old McDonald Had a Farm"

I told him and he told her.
Who told you?
I told him and he told her.
Who told you?

I told him.
He told her.
He knows. She knows.
Everybody here knows.

I told him and he told her.
Who told you?

    You told him and he told me.
    Who told her?
    You told him and he told me.
    Who told her?

    You told him.
    He told her.
    He knows. She knows.
    Everybody here knows.

    You told him and he told her.
    Who told you?

✦ This song provides examples of simple past affirmative and negative statements. Call attention to the simple past forms of the irregular verbs *ring, write,* and *give (rang, wrote, gave)* in affirmative statements and the negative forms with *didn't: didn't answer, didn't write, didn't wear.*

✦ Point out that the pronunciation of the base form of the verb *read* in the negative *didn't read* is different from the affirmative past form *read.*

# 26 The Telephone Rang, but I Didn't Answer It

Melody: "The Old Gray Mare"

The telephone rang, but I didn't answer it.
I didn't answer it.
I didn't answer it.
The telephone rang, but I didn't answer it.
I didn't answer at all.

I wrote him a letter, but he didn't answer it.
He didn't answer it.
He didn't answer it.
I wrote him a letter, but he didn't answer it.
He didn't answer at all.

She gave him a sweater, but he didn't wear it.
He didn't wear it.
He didn't wear it.
She gave him a sweater, but he didn't wear it.
He didn't wear it at all.

He gave her a book, but she didn't read it.
She didn't read it.
She didn't read it.
He gave her a book, but she didn't read it.
She didn't read it at all.

The telephone rang, but I didn't answer it.
I didn't answer it.
I didn't answer it.
The telephone rang, but I didn't answer it.
I didn't answer at all.

✦ This song opens in the simple
present (*All the girls in
Cucamonga love the boys in San
Jose.*) and then moves to the
past (*He was. . .He grew up. . .He
was. . . He grew old. . .*).

✦ Call attention to the use of
the prepositions *in* and *on* (*in
Cucamonga, in San Jose, on a
bright September day*).

✦ Have students listen for and
practice:

— the z sound of the plural
  ending in *girls, boys, years;*

— the rhyming sounds of
  *U.S.A./San Jose, day/U.S.A.*

# 27 Cucamonga, California

Melody: "My Darling Clementine"

Cucamonga, California.
Cucamonga, U.S.A.
All the girls in Cucamonga
love the boys in San Jose.

Cucamonga, California.
Cucamonga, U.S.A.
All the boys in Cucamonga
love the girls in San Jose.

He was born in Cucamonga
on a bright September day.
He grew up in Cucamonga,
Cucamonga, U.S.A.

Cucamonga every evening.
Cucamonga every day.
He was there in Cucamonga.
Cucamonga, U.S.A.

Ninety years in Cucamonga.
Cucamonga, U.S.A.
He grew old in Cucamonga.
Cucamonga, U.S.A.

Cucamonga, California.
Cucamonga, U.S.A.
All the boys in Cucamonga
love the girls in San Jose.

# 28 The Chocolate Cake Song

✦ This song provides practice in the simple past form of the irregular verbs *eat, get,* and *drink* (*ate, got,* and *drank*). It also illustrates the use of the present tense of the verbs *think* and *need* as well as the future with *be going to* in *I think I'm going to die.* Call attention to the use of the indefinite article *a* with count nouns (*a chocolate cake, a stomachache, a pizza pie*) versus *some* with noncount nouns (*some herbal tea, some sympathy*).

✦ Have students listen to and practice the rhyming sounds in *cake/stomachache, pie/die, tea/me, sympathy/pharmacy.*

Melody: "Santa Lucia"

I ate a chocolate cake.
I got a stomachache.
I ate a pizza pie.
I think I'm going to die.
I drank some herbal tea.
I think it poisoned me.
I need some sympathy.
I need a pharmacy.

**NOTES**

✦ This song provides an example of the use of the third-person singular in the simple present. Point out the *s* sound of this form in the verb *speaks*.

✦ **He Speaks English** also provides practice in the difficult sounds of the adverb *fluently* and the contrasting *v* and *w* sounds in the expression *very well*.

Melody: "Good Night, Ladies"

He speaks English.
She speaks English.
They speak English.
They speak it very well.

He speaks English fluently, fluently, fluently.
He speaks English fluently.
He speaks it very well.

He speaks English.
She speaks English.
They speak English.
They speak it very well.

✦ This song provides practice in the simple past form of the irregular verbs *buy, leave, lose, find,* and *take* (*bought, left, lost, found,* and *took*). It also illustrates the use of *I'm sure/I think* and the future with *be going to* as in *I think/I'm sure it's going to rain.*

✦ Have students listen for and practice:

— the conversational reduction of *going to* to *gonna;*

— the linking of the final consonant + vowel sounds in *bought a, left it, red umbrella, an old, that old;*

— the prepositional phrases *on the train, on the sidewalk, near the train.*

# 30 The Red Umbrella

Melody: "Auld Lang Syne"

I bought a red umbrella,
but I left it on the train.
I lost my red umbrella.
Now I think it's going to rain.

I think it's going to rain today.
I'm sure it's going to rain.
I wish I hadn't left
my red umbrella
on the train.

I found an old umbrella
on the sidewalk, near the train.
I took that old umbrella,
'cause I think it's going to rain.

I think it's going to rain today.
I'm sure it's going to rain.
I wish I hadn't left
my red umbrella
on the train.

# Part III

## New Chants

◆ This chant provides practice in the simple present to indicate habitual activities. It also offers practice in the affirmative addition *So do I* to express agreement.

◆ Have students listen for and practice the *s* sound of the third-person singular ending in *he likes* and *he eats*.

# 31 Pizza Chant

Pizza, pizza, pizza pie.
    He likes pizza.
    So do I.
Pizza with tomatoes,
ham, and cheese.
    I'd like a slice of pizza, please.

Pizza with meatballs, sausage, too.
    I'd like a large one.
    How about you?

Pineapple pizza?
That's OK.
He eats pizza every day.

Pizza, pizza, pizza pie.
    He likes pizza.
    So do I.

# 32 Are You Free for Lunch?

✦ This chant provides examples of casual invitations: *Are you free for lunch/dinner?*, *Let's grab a sandwich*. The chant also provides models for accepting or rejecting invitations: *Not today, How about tomorrow?, That's OK, That sounds fine, That's all right, That sounds great, Not right now*. Also point out the use of *How about* for making suggestions: *How about tomorrow?, How about eight?*

✦ Have students listen for and practice:

— the rising intonation of the Yes/No questions *Are you free for lunch?*, *Are you free for dinner?*, *Can you take a break?*;

— the reduced sound of the initial *o* in *today, tomorrow,* and *tonight*;

— the contractions *That's, it'll, Let's, I've.*

Are you free for lunch?
>Not today.
>How about tomorrow?
That's OK,
but it'll have to be early.
>Let's meet at noon.
That sounds fine.
See you soon.

Are you free for dinner?
>Not tonight.
>How about tomorrow?
That's all right.

I feel like a pizza.
>That sounds great!
>When can we meet?
How about eight?

Let's grab a sandwich.
Can you take a break?
>Not right now.
>I've got a deadline to make.

✦ This chant provides practice in the simple present to indicate either a permanent condition (*I love hamburgers.*) or a habitual, everyday activity (*They eat hamburgers every day.*).

✦ It also provides practice in several affirmative additions to express agreement: *I do, too, So does he/she, So do we/they.* Also point out the expression *Not me* to indicate disagreement.

✦ Have students listen for and practice:

— the *z* sound of the plural *s* in *hamburgers, cheeseburgers, veggie-burgers;*

— the *z* sound of the third-person *s* ending in *he/she loves;*

— the blending of the final *z* sound in *does* with the initial *sh* sound in *she* in the phrase *does she.*

# 33 The Hamburger Chant

I love hamburgers.
    I do, too.
I love cheeseburgers.
    I do, too.
I love veggie-burgers.
    Not me.
    I love hamburgers.
So does he.
He loves hamburgers.
    So does she.
    She loves hamburgers.
So do we.
We love hamburgers.
    So do they.
    They eat hamburgers
    every day.

# 34 I Wonder What Time It Is

**NOTES**

✦ This chant provides practice in language commonly used when responding to good news (*Oh, good!*) and to bad news (*Oh, no!*).

✦ Have students listen for and practice:

— the long, stressed sound of *time* in the opening line *I wonder what time it is;*

— the contractions *I'm* and *it's.*

✦ This chant provides an excellent model for students to practice thinking in English in their daily lives. Suggest to students that when they wake up in the morning, the first thing they should do is to say, "I wonder what time it is!" and then look at their clock for the actual time and say either, "Oh, good! It's only ____ ." or "Oh, no! It's ____ ." Have students practice the models for a week, and then ask if it helped them to think in English.

I wonder what time it is.
I wonder what time it is.
I hope it's not late.
I hope it's not late.
I wonder what time it is.

    Oh, good! It's only eight.
    I'm not late. I'm not late.
    Oh, good! It's only eight.
    I'm not late!

I wonder what time it is.
I wonder what time it is.
I hope it's not late.
I hope it's not late.
I wonder what time it is.

    Oh, no! It's eight o'clock.
    I'm late!
    I'm late!
    Oh, no! It's eight o'clock.
    I'm late.

# 35 My Computer's Down

✦ This chant provides useful vocabulary relating to the frustrations of someone whose computer has broken down. Call attention to the expressions of defeat and despair: *I'm through, I quit, This is it, I've had enough, It's really tough.* Also point out the use of *will* to ask for advice in *What'll I do?*

✦ **My Computer's Down** also provides practice in simple present *Wh*-questions with *What* and *Why.* Have students listen for and practice the falling intonation pattern of these questions: *What's the matter?, Why the frown?, What's the problem?, What'll I do?*

✦ Have students listen for and practice:

— the contractions *What's, computer's, What'll, I've, I'm, it's;*

— the rhyming words: *nurse/worse, do/through, quit/it, enough/tough, do/you.*

What's the matter? Why the frown?
What's the problem?

    My computer's down.
    Call the doctor. Call the nurse.
    Things are bad
    and getting worse.

    My computer's down.
    What'll I do?
    My computer's down.
    I'm through.

    My computer's down.
    I quit.
    My computer's down.
    This is it!

I quit. I'm through.
I've had enough.
My computer's down.
It's really tough!

    My computer's down.
    What'll I do?
    Listen to me! I'm talking to you.

# 36 The Answering Machine Blues

◆ This chant provides the language often heard as the recorded greeting on a telephone-answering machine. Call attention to the use of the command form (*Leave your name and number.*) and the future with *will* to express a promise (*We'll call you right back…*).

◆ Explain that the expression *We'll get right back* means "We'll return your call very soon."

◆ Have students listen for and practice the conversational reduction of *and* to *en* in *name and number*.

Sorry, we're out.
Leave your name and number.
Sorry, we're out.
Leave your name and number.
Sorry, we're out.
Leave your name and number.
We'll call you right back
just as soon as we can.

Your call is important.
Leave your name and number.
Your call is important.
Leave your name and number.

Leave your name and number
at the sound of the beep,
and we'll get right back
just as soon as we can.

✦ This chant provides useful, high-frequency vocabulary used when placing an order in an informal restaurant—for example: *I'd like a…, Coffee, please. Dark, no sugar. Large, please.* Also presented is a variety of questions asked by servers—for example: *What kind of…?, Anything to drink?, Milk and sugar?, Large or small?, To stay or to go?*

✦ Have students listen to and practice the conversational reduction of *going to* to *gonna*.

# 37 Fast Food

What are you going to have?
 I'd like a grilled cheese sandwich.
What kind of bread?
 Rye bread.
What kind of cheese?
 American cheese.
 I'd like a grilled cheese sandwich on rye bread
 and a side order of french fries.
Anything to drink?
 Coffee, please.
What kind of coffee?
 Excuse me?
We have Italian espresso, decaf cappuccino,
café au lait, café latte …
 Plain old American coffee, please.
Milk and sugar?
 Dark, no sugar.
Large or small?
 Large, please.
To stay or to go?
 What did you say?
To stay or to go?
 I don't know.
Are you going to have it here,
or are you going to take it home?
To stay or to go?
 I don't know.

# 38 E-mail Boogie

✦ This chant provides examples of the simple present used with the time expression *every day* to show a repeated action. It also practices short expressions of agreement: *I do, too, So do they, So does she. So do we.*

✦ Have students listen for and practice:

— the *z* sound of the third-person singular marker *s* in *he/she loves;*

— the rhyming patterns in *too/you* and *they/day.*

I love E-mail.
    I do, too.
    I love E-mail.
    So will you.

We love E-mail.
    So do they.
    They get E-mail
    every day.

He loves E-mail.
    So does she.
    She loves E-mail.
So do we.

We love E-mail.
    So do they.
    They get E-mail
    every day.

# 39 He's a Wonderful Dentist

✦ This chant illustrates the contrasting sounds of *he's* (the contraction of the subject pronoun *he + is*) versus the possessive adjective *his*.

✦ Have students listen for and practice the pronunciation of the descriptive adjectives in the chant: *wonderful, very good, marvelous, fabulous, bright, excellent,* and *brilliant.* Point out the use of the indefinite article *a/an (a brilliant student, an excellent teacher).*

He's a wonderful dentist.
His name is Danny.

She's a very good patient.
Her name is Annie.

He's a marvelous singer.
His name is Bill.

She's a fabulous dancer.
Her name is Jill.

She's a very good writer.
Her name is Sherri.

He's a very bright lawyer.
His name is Larry.

She's an excellent teacher.
Her name is Sandy.

He's a brilliant student.
His name is Andy.

# 40 Argument Chant

✦ This chant provides examples of Yes/No questions with *be* (*Is he a student?*) and with other verbs (*Does he study every day?*). Remind students that Yes/No questions almost always have a rising intonation. Also call attention to the affirmative and negative short answers to these Yes/No questions, such as *Yes, I am/No, I'm not* and *Yes, he does/No, he doesn't*.

✦ Call attention to the frequency adverbs *always* and *usually*, pointing out that they come after the verb *be*: *Is he always late to class?*, *Is he usually on time?*

✦ Note that some of the stanzas of this chant call for four voices, which can be performed either by four individuals or by four groups.

Is he a student?
    Yes, he is.
Is he a *good* student?
    Yes, he is.
        No, he isn't.
            Yes, I am!

Does he study every day?
    Yes, he does.
        No, he doesn't.
    Yes, he does.
        No, he doesn't.
            Yes, I do!

Does he write very well?
    Yes, he does.
        No, he doesn't.
            Yes, I do!

Does he speak very well?
    Yes, he does.
        No, he doesn't.
            Yes, I do!

Is he *always* late to class?
    No, he isn't.
        Yes, he is.
            No, I'm not!

Is he usually on time?
    Yes, he is.
        No, he isn't.
            Yes, I am!

✦ This chant provides practice in simple present statements using the following two patterns: Subject + *be* + adjective *(She's nice.)* and Subject + verb + object *(I like her.)*.

✦ Have students listen for and practice the intensifiers *really* and *very*, giving them the appropriate amount of enthusiasm.

# 41 She's Nice. I Like Her.

She's nice. I like her.
She's nice. I like her.
I really like her very much.
She's really very nice.

He's nice. I like him.
He's nice. I like him.
I really like him very much.
He's really very nice.

They're nice. I like them.
They're nice. I like them.
I really like them very much.
They're really very nice.

# 42 I Don't Like Her. I Can't Help It.

✦ This chant illustrates the use of negative statements in the simple present (*I don't like her, I can't help it,* etc.). It provides practice in language commonly used to express dislike of someone: *She drives me crazy, She drives me nuts, I can't stand her.*

✦ Have students listen for and practice the pronunciation of the negative contractions *don't* and *can't*.

✦ Point out that the chant reflects the type of talking about someone that would take place when the person isn't present.

I don't like her.
I can't help it.
I can't stand her.
I don't like her.
She really irritates me.
I can't help it.
She drives me crazy.
She drives me nuts.

I can't stand her.
I don't like her at all.
She really irritates me.
I can't help it.
I don't like her.
I. don't like her at all.
I can't help it.
I can't stand her.

I hate to talk to her.
I can't stand her.
I hate to listen to her.
I can't stand her.
She really irritates me.
I can't help it.
She drives me crazy.
She drives me nuts.

✦ This chant illustrates the use of affirmative and negative statements in the simple past (*I spoke very slowly, I didn't speak fast*). Point out the irregular past form of the verb *speak* (*spoke*) in the affirmative past statement in contrast to the use of *didn't* + base form (*speak*) in the negative past statement.

✦ Explain that *couldn't* is the negative past form of the modal *can*.

✦ Have students listen for and practice the adverbs *well, fast, quickly*, and the intensifiers *very* and *so*.

# 43 Everyone Spoke English at the Party Last Night

Everyone spoke English at the party last night.
Some people spoke it very well.
I tried to join their conversation,
but I couldn't understand them very well.
They spoke so quickly. They spoke so fast.
I couldn't understand them very well.
I tried to answer their questions,
but they couldn't understand me very well.
I spoke very slowly. I didn't speak fast,
but they didn't understand me very well.
I met a lot of people at the party last night,
but I didn't understand them very well.

# 44 Fresh Fish

✦ This chant provides practice in *Wh-* questions using the contracted form of *will: Who'll catch it?, Who'll cook it?, Who'll eat it?* Point out that the full form of *will* is used in the short responses *She will, He will, We will.*

✦ Have students listen for and practice the pronunciation of:

— the repeated *f* sounds in *Fresh fish for …* ;

— the final *ch* sound in *lunch* and *munch.*

Fresh fish.
Fresh fish for breakfast.
Fresh fish.
Fresh fish for lunch.

Fresh fish for breakfast.
Fresh fish for lunch.
Fresh fish for dinner.
Munch, munch, munch, munch!

Fresh fish.
Fresh fish.
Fresh fish for breakfast.
Fresh fish.

Who'll catch it?
    She will.
Who'll cook it?
    He will.
Who'll eat it?
    We will.
    Fresh fish.

Fresh fish for breakfast.
Fresh fish for lunch.
Fresh fish for dinner.
Munch, munch, munch, munch!

✦ This chant offers a wide
variety of food-related
vocabulary.

✦ **Pete Eats Meat** provides
practice in affirmative and
negative statements in the
simple present—for example:
*Pete eats meat. He doesn't eat
fish.* It also practices the short
responses *I do, too* and *So do I*
to indicate agreement.

✦ Have students listen for and
practice:

— the *z* sound of the plural *s*
ending in *meatballs, oysters,
onions, vegetables*;

— the *iz* sound of the plural *es*
ending in *sandwiches*;

— the *sh* sound in *fish, shell,
shellfish, fresh*;

— the *ch* sound in *sandwich,
lunch*;

— the rhyming words *Pete/meat,
Trish/fish, Marian/vegetarian,
stew/too, pie/I.*

# 45 Pete Eats Meat

Pete eats meat.
He doesn't eat fish.
Pete likes meat, red meat.
Meat for breakfast.
    Bacon, sausage.
Meat for lunch.
    Ham sandwiches.
Meat for dinner.
    Meatloaf, meatballs.
Pete loves meat,
red meat.

Trish eats fish.
She doesn't eat meat.
Trish loves shellfish.
    Shrimp cocktail.
Fresh shellfish.
    Clams, scallops,
    oysters on the half-shell,
    lobster stew.
Trish eats shellfish.
Fresh shellfish.
Trish loves shellfish.
I do, too.

Marian's a vegetarian.
She doesn't eat meat.
She doesn't eat fish.
Marian's a vegetarian.
She eats vegetables every day.
    Broccoli pizza, mushroom stew.
    Garlic soup with onions, too.
    Eggplant, carrots, cauliflower pie.
She loves vegetables.
So do I!

# 46 My PC

✦ This chant provides vocabulary items associated with the world of computers: *cursor, keyboard, monitor, mouse,* etc.

✦ Have students listen for and practice:

— the contracted forms of *There is (There's), Where is (Where's),* and *It is (It's);*

— the definite article *the* in *the CD* and *the power supply* versus the indefinite article *a* in *a personal computer;*

— the rhyming sounds of *mouse/house, CD/me, try/supply.*

Cursor, keyboard,
monitor, mouse.
There's a personal computer
in my house.

Diskette, disk drive.
Where's the CD?
My personal computer
is looking for me.

Cursor, keyboard,
monitor, mouse.
I like that PC
in my house.

It's user-friendly,
if you try.
But don't forget to switch on
the power supply.

✦ This chant provides examples of vocabulary items related to a hospital setting: *crutches, cast, wheelchair, stretcher, ambulance,* etc.

✦ Call attention to the prepositions *in* and *on* as they're used in the chant: *on crutches, in a cast, in a wheelchair, on a stretcher, in bed, in an ambulance, on a one-way street.* Point out that there is no article in the expression *in bed.*

✦ Have students listen for and practice:

— the indefinite articles *a* in *a cast, a blanket, a pillow* and *an* in *an ambulance;*

— the rhyming patterns of *cast/fast, bed/head, Pete/street, flu/too.*

# 47 Hospital Chant

Kenny's on crutches.
Cathy's in a cast.
Willie's in a wheelchair,
moving fast.

Sally's on a stretcher.
Bobby's in bed.
The nurse has a blanket and a pillow for his head.

Andy's in an ambulance.
So is Pete.
They were driving too fast
on a one-way street.

Freddy has a fever.
Frankie has the flu.
The nurse is getting nervous,
'cause the doctor's coughing, too.

# 48 I Hate Voice Mail

## NOTES

✦ This chant presents the language commonly used in voice-mail greetings. It also provides an example of strong language used to express extreme dislike or irritation: *I hate....*

✦ **I Hate Voice Mail** also provides practice in conditional statements with *if (If you're calling from a touch-tone phone...)* and command forms *(Press... Just remember...).*

✦ Have students listen for and practice the rhyming patterns of *do/too, touch-tone/phone, call/all, spare/care.*

I hate voice mail.
I really do.
I hate voice mail.
You will, too.

"If you're calling from
a touch-tone phone, press 1.
If you don't have a touch-tone phone, say 'Two.'
If you're calling from a mobile phone, press 8.
You can dance to the music while you
wait, wait, wait.
Press 4 for the list of people to call.
Press 5 if you don't have a name at all.
Press 6 if you have lots of time to spare.
Press 7 if you want to. We don't care!"

You hate your voice mail.
We know you do.
Just remember that your voice mail
hates you, too!

✦ This chant provides contracted affirmative and negative examples of the future with *will* as well as questions using the full form. Have students listen for and practice the examples: *Will it rain today, or will it snow?, We won't have rain, We'll probably get a hurricane.* Also point out the use of *probably* to express strong possibility.

✦ **Weather Report** also provides practice in the use of *don't* in the negative command form *(Don't listen to the forecasters.)* and in simple present negative statements *(They don't know.).*

✦ Have students listen for and practice the rhyming sounds of *snow/know, rain/hurricane, get/wet.*

# 49 Weather Report

Will it rain today,
or will it snow?
Don't listen to the forecasters.
They don't know.

When the weatherman says,
"We won't have rain,"
we'll probably get a hurricane.

He promised us sunshine,
and what did we get?
We got very, very, wet.

# 50  I Like the City

✦ This chant provides examples of the simple present of the verbs *love* and *like* followed by noun phrases. Point out the use of the definite article *the* in the following noun phrases, and have students listen for and practice them: *the city, the buildings, the sky, the rhythm, the city street, the music, the beat, the jazz, the park, the dark.*

✦ Have students listen for and practice:

— the *z* sound of the plural *s* in *buildings, taxis;*

— the *s* sound of the plural marker in *lights;*

— the rhyming patterns of *too/do, sky/I, street/beat, park/dark, lights/night.*

I like the city.
> I do, too.
> There's so much to see.
> So much to do.

Look at the buildings
touching the sky.
I love the city.
> So do I.

I like the rhythm on the city street.
> I like the music.
> I like the beat.

I like the jazz. I like the park.
I like to window-shop in the dark.

Yellow taxis.
Neon lights.
My favorite city
is up all night.

# Part IV

## New Songs

# 51 Harry Loves Mary

✦ This song illustrates useful vocabulary for describing relationships, such as *loves, is in love with, doesn't care,* and *can't stand.*

✦ The song also provides examples of compound sentences with *but*. Point out that the conjunction *but* is used to contrast two different ideas or contrary information (*Harry loves Mary, but Mary loves Jim.*).

✦ **Harry Loves Mary** also offers examples of simple present affirmative and negative statements in the third-person singular using the verb *love: He loves her, but she doesn't love him.* Point out the *z* sound of the third-person *s* in the affirmative form and the use of *doesn't* + the base form of the verb in negative statements.

✦ Have students listen for and practice:

— the subject pronouns *he* and *she* and the corresponding object pronouns *him* and *her;*

— the rhyming patterns of *Jim/him/Tim, care/fair, Fay/Day.*

Harry loves Mary,
but Mary loves Jim.
He loves her,
but she doesn't love him.

Jimmy loves Sally,
but Sally loves Tim.
Tim's in love with Jenny,
but she can't stand him.

Jack's in love with Penny,
but she doesn't care.
She's in love with Benny.
Love isn't fair.

Benny doesn't love her.
He's in love with Fay.
Happy Valentine's Day. Oh, yeah!
Happy Valentine's Day!

# 52 Catching Fish in Canada

◆ This song provides examples of the present continuous with a wide variety of action verbs: *catching, cooking, eating, selling, working, dancing, climbing, building, racing, studying, drinking, waking up, writing, reading, selling,* and *buying.*

◆ Call attention to the special meaning of the preposition *on* in the phrase *on music, art, and dance,* where it means "about." Also point out that *fish* is used as a noncount noun in the song.

◆ Have students listen for and practice the rhyming sounds of *Spain/Maine, Brazil/hill, Rome/Nome, Seoul/roll, France/dance, day/L.A.* Explain that the city of Los Angeles, California, is often referred to as L.A., pronounced as separate letters: "L-A."

Oh, they're catching fish in Canada.
They're cooking fish in Spain.
They're eating fish in Boston
and selling fish in Maine.

They're working hard in Singapore.
They're dancing in Brazil.
Up north in San Francisco,
they're climbing up a hill.

They're building cars in Tokyo.
They're racing cars in Rome.
The students in Alaska
are studying in Nome.

They're drinking tea in London.
They're eating rice in Seoul.
They're waking up in Washington
with coffee and a roll.

They're writing books in England.
They're reading books in France.
They're selling books in Switzerland
on music, art, and dance.

They're buying books in China
and reading night and day.
The kids are reading comic books
on the beaches in L.A.
Oh, yeah, the kids are reading comic books
on the beaches in L.A.

✦ This song provides practice in the simple present third-person singular form of the verbs *wear* and *look*. Call attention to and have students practice the contrasting final sounds in *wears* (*z* sound) versus *looks* (*s* sound).

✦ **The Blue Jeans Blues** also provides examples of prepositional phrases with the names of the seasons: *in the winter, in the fall, in the summer.* Point out that the article *the* is sometimes omitted.

✦ Have students substitute the words *he* and *him* for *she* and *her* in various repetitions of this song.

# 53 The Blue Jeans Blues

She wears jeans, blue jeans.
She wears jeans, blue jeans.
She looks good in her blue jeans.
She looks good in her blue jeans.
She wears jeans in the winter, jeans in the fall,
jeans in the summer, any time at all.
She wears jeans, blue jeans.
She wears jeans, blue jeans.

She wears a T-shirt with her blue jeans.
She wears a T-shirt with her blue jeans.
She looks good in her blue jeans.
She looks good in her blue jeans.
She looks very, very good in her T-shirt and jeans.
She looks very, very good in her jeans.

# 54 Bobby's Back

✦ This song provides practice in simple present affirmative statements with the verb *be*. Have students listen for and practice the contractions with pronouns or nouns and *be: I'm, we're, you're, everybody's, Bobby's.*

✦ Point out the use of the intensifier *so* with the adjective *happy (I'm so happy…).*

✦ Encourage students to substitute their own names for *Bobby* in various repetitions of the song.

Bobby's back.
I'm so happy that
Bobby's back.
We're so happy that
Bobby's here.
Everybody's happy that
Bobby's back again.

Bobby's here.
We're so happy that
Bobby's here.
We're so happy that
Bobby's back.
We're so happy that
Bobby's back again.

Bobby's back.
I'm so happy that
Bobby's back.
You're so happy that
Bobby's back.
Everybody's happy that
Bobby's back again.

# 55 She Thinks About Him

**NOTES**

✦ This song provides examples of the simple present to indicate habitual action, focusing on third-person singular forms with the subject pronoun *she*.

✦ Call attention to the time expressions *all the time, in the morning*, and *in the evening*. Also point out the use of *about* in the verbal phrases *think about, talk about*, and *dream about*.

✦ Encourage students to invent their own variations of this song—for example: *He thinks about her, I think about him, Mom thinks about me*.

She thinks about him.
She thinks about him.
She thinks about him all the time.

She thinks about him.
She talks about him.
She dreams about him all the time.

She thinks about him in the morning,
him, in the evening.
She thinks about him all the time.
She talks about him in the morning,
him, in the evening.
She talks about him.
She thinks about him.
She dreams about him all the time.

# Part V

## *Carolina Shout in Performance*

NOTE: Carolyn Graham uses the name Carolina Shout when she performs ragtime piano concerts. The songs included here are for students and teachers alike to have fun with and are not pedagogical in nature.

## 56 Tokyo Business Blues

Woke up in Roppongi.
Blues were in my bed.
Woke up in Roppongi.
Blues were in my bed.
Went to see the doctor, baby.
This is what he said.

"You've got the business blues, Oooh.
You've got those business blues.
Business blues, Oooh.
You've got those business blues.
I can see it in your face.
You've got a bad, bad case
of the business blues."

Going to Osaka.
Can't you feel the pain.
Business blues are riding, baby,
on the bullet train.

Business blues, Oooh.
I've got those business blues.
Gotta get some money, honey.
Gotta lose those business blues.

## 57 There's a Light at the End of the Tunnel

Mama told me life was tough.
Mama told me life was hard.
There'd be days when the sun would never shine.
Mama promised me that I
would be happy by and by.
There's a light in the tunnel up ahead.
But when that light up ahead
in the tunnel is a freight train,
Mama taught me never to look back. Don't look back.
When that light up ahead
in the tunnel is a freight train,
be sure you're on the train and not the track.

Don't just stand there in the rain.
Get yourself up on the train.
Mama taught me never to look back. Don't look back.
When that light up ahead
in the tunnel is a freight train,
be sure you're on the train and not the track.

Carolina Shout

# 58 Put Me Through to Elvis

Help me operator, gotta give your all.
Put me through to Elvis. This is a long-distance call.
Gotta talk to Elvis. Call him up tonight.
Gotta talk to Elvis, 'cause things aren't going right.

My life is down to empty.
My heart is broke in two.
My dream is torn to pieces.
Nothing I can do.
Put me through to Elvis.
Get him on the line.
Put me through to Elvis.
He was a friend of mine.

Nothing left to live for.
My world has come apart.
No one here can help me
mend my broken heart.
I need someone to hold me.
Trying not to fall.
Put me through to Elvis, Mama.
This is a long, long-distance call.

Nothing left to live for.
My world has come apart.
No one here can help me
mend my broken heart.
I need someone to hold me.
Trying not to fall.
Put me through to Elvis, Mama.
This is a long-distance call.
Put me through to Elvis, Mama.
This is a long-distance call.

**Note:** The line *My heart is broke in two* uses poetic
license. The standard English usage is *My heart is
broken in two*.

## 59 The Cell Phone Blues

Call me in the morning.
Call me late at night.
Call me at the office, baby.
That's all right. Just as long as you
call me, call me.
Call me on the telephone.

Call me on your cell phone, baby.
Call me when you're all alone.

Now you can phone me on the sidewalk,
phone me in the hall,
call me from your cell phone, baby,
anytime at all. Just as long as you call me,
call me, call me on the telephone.

Call me on your cell phone, baby.
Call me when you're all alone.

Carolina Shout

# 60 Dogstar Shining

You'll be all right
all through the night.
Dogstar shining,
shining so bright.

Nothing can harm you
under his light.
Dogstar shining tonight.

Nothing can hurt you.
Nothing to fear.
Nothing can harm you.
Dogstar is near.

Nothing can hurt you
under his light.
Dogstar shining tonight.

**Note:** Dogstar is the common name for Sirius, the brightest star in the heavens. Dogstar is a reassuring, friendly presence for sailors on the high seas.

# Part VI

## Exercises for Chants and Songs

NOTE TO THE TEACHER: See the section entitled *The Exercises* on page viii for suggestions about presenting the exercises.

# 1 Sh! Sh! Baby's Sleeping!

Listen carefully as your teacher reads the sentences below. Then listen again as your teacher repeats them. Fill in the blanks with the correct words. Check your answers in the Answer Key, page 96.

1. The _____ _____ sleeping.

2. _____ the _____ sleeping?

3. What _____ _____ say?

4. The _____ _____ sleeping.

5. What _____ _____ say?

# 2 Do You Know Mary?

Answer the questions below. Use information from the chant. Use complete sentences in your answers. If you need more space, use a separate piece of paper. Check your answers in the Answer Key, page 96.

1. What is Mary's last name? _____

2. Who is Betty? _____

3. Who is Sue? _____

4. What is the name of Mary's aunt? _____

5. What is the name of Mary's husband? _____

## 3 Tall Trees

Listen carefully as your teacher reads the sentences below. Then listen again as your teacher repeats them. Fill in the blanks with the correct words. Check your answers in the Answer Key, page 96.

1. The _____ of California _____ _____ _____

   sight with the _____, _____ trees.

2. The _____ _____ northern California _____

   very, very _____.

3. Look _____ _____ tall _____!

4. _____ _____ _____ redwood _____. _____ huge.

5. _____ _____ _____ tree _____ _____?

   _____ _____ California redwood tree.

## 4 Rain

Fill in the blanks below with the correct words. Use the information from the chant. Check your answers in the Answer Key, page 96.

1. It was _____ hard.

2. It was falling on _____ shoes.

3. I got soaking _____.

4. The rain _____ warm.

5. It reminded _____ of _____.

## 5 Major Decisions

Ask your partner the following questions and write the answers below or on a separate piece of paper. Use complete sentences.

1. How do you like your coffee? _____

2. How do you like your tea? _____

3. How do you like your steak? _____

4. How do you like your eggs? _____

5. Do you like omelets? _____

## 6 Banker's Wife's Blues

Listen to your teacher read five questions. Then listen again and write the questions below. Check your answers in the Answer Key, page 96.

1. _____

2. _____

3. _____

4. _____

5. _____

Now work with a classmate and answer the questions above using the information from the chant. Check your answers in the Answer Key, page 96.

1. _____

2. _____

3. _____

4. _____

5. _____

## 7 My Feet Hurt!

Look at the complaints below. Write a suggestion or solution next to each complaint. Use the information from the chant. If you need more space, use a separate piece of paper. Check your answers in the Answer Key, page 96.

1. My feet hurt! _____

2. It's hot in here! _____

3. It's cold in here! _____

4. My hands are cold! _____

## 8 Departure and Return Home

Listen to your teacher read five sentences. Then listen again and write the sentences below. Check your answers in the Answer Key, page 96.

1. _____

2. _____

3. _____

4. _____

5. _____

## 9 Panic on Being Late

Listen carefully as your teacher reads the sentences below. Then listen again as your teacher repeats them. Fill in the blanks with the correct words. Check your answers in the Answer Key, page 96.

1. _____ time _____ it?

2. Hurry _____ ! Hurry _____ !

3. We're _____ to _____ late.

4. _____ late, _____ late, I'm _____ late!

5. I _____ have time _____ _____ to you

_____ .

## 10 Personal Questions

Listen to your teacher read five questions. Then listen again and write the questions below. Check your answers in the Answer Key, page 96.

1. _____

2. _____

3. _____

4. _____

5. _____

Now work with a classmate and write five more personal questions together.

6. _____

7. _____

8. _____

9. _____

10. _____

## 11 Mama Knows Best

Listen to your teacher read five questions. Then listen again and write the sentences below. Check your answers in the Answer Key, page 96.

1. _____

2. _____

3. _____

4. _____

5. _____

Now work with a classmate and write five more sentences giving advice using *shouldn't* or *ought to*.

6. _____

7. _____

8. _____

9. _____

10. _____

## 12 On the Rocks

Listen carefully as your teacher reads the sentences below. Then listen again as your teacher repeats them. Fill in the blanks with the correct words. Check your answers in the Answer Key, page 96.

1. You never _____ to _____.

2. He never _____ to _____.

3. He just _____ around and _____ TV.

4. She _____ _____ _____ me.

5. What _____ you _____?

## 13 Taking Credit

Listen to your teacher read five questions. Then listen again and write the questions below. Check your answers in the Answer Key, page 96.

1. _____
2. _____
3. _____
4. _____
5. _____

Now work with a classmate and write five questions and answers about things that belong to people in your class.

**Example:** Whose pen is that? It's Kim's.

6. _____
7. _____
8. _____
9. _____
10. _____

## 14 It's Got to Be Somewhere

Listen to your teacher read five sentences. Then listen again and write the sentences below. Check your answers in the Answer Key, page 96.

1. _____
2. _____
3. _____
4. _____
5. _____

## 15 Twelve Cans of Tuna Fish Rag

Answer the questions below. Use the information from the chant.
If you need more space, use a separate piece of paper. Check your
answers in the Answer Key, page 97.

1. What does she eat? _____

2. What kind of fish does she eat? _____

3. How many cans of tuna does she eat? _____

4. How often does she eat those twelve cans? _____

5. Is that a lot of fish? _____


## 16 I Gave It Away

Listen to your teacher read five questions. Then listen again and
write the questions below. Check your answers in the Answer Key,
page 97.

1. _____

2. _____

3. _____

4. _____

5. _____

Now work with a classmate and answer the questions above using
the information from the chant. Check your answers in the Answer
Key, page 97.

1. _____

2. _____

3. _____

4. _____

5. _____

## 17 Selfish

Listen carefully as your teacher reads the sentences below. Then listen again as your teacher repeats them. Fill in the blanks with the correct words. Check your answers in the Answer Key, page 97.

1. This _____ mine! That's _____!

2. Don't touch _____! Get your _____!

3. What _____ you doing with _____?

4. What's _____ is _____.

5. What's _____ is _____.

## 18 Easy Solutions

Listen to your teacher read five complaints. Then listen again and write the complaints below. Check your answers in the Answer Key, page 97.

1. _____

2. _____

3. _____

4. _____

5. _____

Now work with a classmate and write solutions to the complaints above using the information from the chant. Check your answers in the Answer Key, page 97.

1. _____

2. _____

3. _____

4. _____

5. _____

## 19 Wake Up! Wake Up!

Listen carefully as your teacher reads the sentences below. Then listen again as your teacher repeats them. Fill in the blanks with the correct words. Check your answers in the Answer Key, page 97.

1. _____ time is it?

2. I _____ want _____ get up.

3. You _____ _____ get up.

4. You _____ get up.

5. You've _____ _____ get up.

## 20 You're Just Like Your Mother

Listen to your teacher read five sentences. Then listen again and write the sentences below. Check your answers in the Answer Key, page 97.

1. _____

2. _____

3. _____

4. _____

5. _____

Now work with a classmate and write negative statements for the sentences above using the information from the chant. Check your answers in the Answer Key, page 97.

1. _____

2. _____

3. _____

4. _____

5. _____

## 21 Native Language

Listen carefully as your teacher reads the sentences below. Then listen again as your teacher repeats them. Fill in the blanks with the correct words. Check your answers in the Answer Key, page 97.

1. He _____ English.

2. _____ _____ she.

3. She _____ _____ in Paris.

4. He _____ _____ in New York.

5. _____ _____ she.

## 22 God Save the TOEFL Test

Answer the questions below. Use the information from the chant. If you need more space, use a separate piece of paper. Check your answers in the Answer Key, page 97.

1. Did you take the TOEFL test? _____

2. Was the test hard? _____

3. Did you get a stomachache? _____

4. Did your eyes fill up with tears? _____

5. What did your teacher promise you? _____

Now ask a classmate question 6 below. If the answer is *yes*, ask question 7. Write your classmate's answer(s) in the space provided.

6. Did you take the TOEFL test? _____

7. Was the test hard? _____

## 23 Henry Wants to Go to Harvard

Listen to your teacher read five questions. Then listen again and write the questions below. Check your answers in the Answer Key, page 97.

1. _____

2. _____

3. _____

4. _____

5. _____

Now work with a classmate and answer the questions above using the information from the chant. Check your answers in the Answer Key, page 97.

1. _____

2. _____

3. _____

4. _____

5. _____

## 24 Love Song

Answer the following questions using the information from the chant. Check your answers in the Answer Key, page 97.

1. Does she love him? Yes, _____.

2. Is she happy? Yes, _____.

3. Does he know it? Yes, _____.

4. Are they lucky? Yes, _____.

5. Will he leave her? Yes, _____.

## 25  I Told Him and He Told Her

Listen to your teacher read five sentences. Then listen again and write the sentences below. Check your answers in the Answer Key, page 98.

1. _____

2. _____

3. _____

4. _____

5. _____


## 26  The Telephone Rang, but I Didn't Answer It

Complete the sentences below. Check your answers in the Answer Key, page 98.

**Example:** I wrote him a letter, but he didn't answer it.

1. She gave him a sweater, but _____.

2. He gave her a book, but _____.

3. They gave us a car, but _____.

4. We gave them a cake, but _____.

5. I gave him a bike, but _____.

## 27 Cucamonga, California

Listen to your teacher read five questions. Then listen again and write the questions below. Check your answers in the Answer Key, page 98.

1. _____

2. _____

3. _____

4. _____

5. _____

Now work with a classmate and answer the questions above using the information from the chant. Check your answers in the Answer Key, page 98.

1. _____

2. _____

3. _____

4. _____

5. _____

## 28 The Chocolate Cake Song

Listen to your teacher read five questions. Then listen again and write the questions below. Check your answers in the Answer Key, page 98.

1. _____

2. _____

3. _____

4. _____

5. _____

Now work with a classmate and answer the questions on page 80 using the information from the chant. Check your answers in the Answer Key, page 98.

1. _____

2. _____

3. _____

4. _____

5. _____

# 29 He Speaks English

Ask your partner the following questions and write the answers below or on a separate piece of paper. Use complete sentences.

1. Does your mother speak English? _____

2. Does your father speak English? _____

3. What language does your mother speak fluently? _____

4. What language does your father speak fluently? _____

5. What language does your best friend speak fluently? _____

# 30 The Red Umbrella

Answer the questions below. Use the information from the chant. Use complete sentences in your answers. Check your answers in the Answer Key, page 98.

1. What did you buy? _____

2. Where did you leave your red umbrella? _____

3. Did you lose your red umbrella? _____

4. Where did you find an old umbrella? _____

5. Do you think it's going to rain today? _____

## 31 Pizza Chant

Ask your partner the following questions and write the answers below or on a separate piece of paper. Use complete sentences. If possible, do a class survey to find out which is the most popular type of pizza.

1. Do you like pizza with cheese? _____

2. Do you like pizza with ham and cheese? _____

3. Do you like pizza with meatballs? _____

4. Do you like pizza with sausage? _____

5. Do you like pineapple pizza? _____


## 32 Are You Free for Lunch?

Listen to your teacher read five sentences. Then listen again and write the sentences below. Check your answers in the Answer Key, page 98.

1. _____

2. _____

3. _____

4. _____

5. _____

## 33  The Hamburger Chant

Ask your partner the following questions and write the answers below or on a separate piece of paper. Use complete sentences. If possible, do a class survey to find out which food people like best: hamburgers, cheeseburgers, veggie-burgers, chicken, or fish.

1. Do you like hamburgers? _____

2. Do you like cheeseburgers? _____

3. Do you like veggie-burgers? _____

4. Do you like chicken? _____

5. Do you like fish? _____

## 34  I Wonder What Time It Is

Listen to your teacher read five sentences. Then listen again and write the sentences below. Check your answers in the Answer Key, page 98.

1. _____

2. _____

3. _____

4. _____

5. _____

## 35 My Computer's Down

Listen carefully as your teacher reads the sentences below. Then
listen again as your teacher repeats them. Fill in the blanks with
the correct words. Check your answers in the Answer Key, page 98.

1. What's _____ matter?

2. _____ the problem?

3. My _____ down.

4. Things are _____ and getting _____.

4. _____ I do?


## 36 The Answering Machine Blues

Listen carefully as your teacher reads the sentences below. Then
listen again as your teacher repeats them. Fill in the blanks with
the correct words. Check your answers in the Answer Key, page 98.

1. _____, we're _____.

2. _____ your name and _____.

3. Your call _____ important.

4. We'll _____ you _____ back.

5. We'll _____ right back just _____ soon _____

    we _____.

## 37 Fast Food

Listen to your teacher read five questions. Then listen again and write the questions below. Check your answers in the Answer Key, page 98.

1. _____
2. _____
3. _____
4. _____
5. _____

Now work with a classmate and answer the questions above using the information from the chant. Check your answers in the Answer Key, page 98.

1. _____
2. _____
3. _____
4. _____
5. _____

## 38 E-mail Boogie

Listen to your teacher read five sentences. Then listen again and write the sentences below. Check your answers in the Answer Key, page 98.

1. _____
2. _____
3. _____
4. _____
5. _____

## 39  He's a Wonderful Dentist

Fill in the blanks below with the correct words. Use the information from the chant. Check your answers in the Answer Key, page 98.

1. He's a wonderful dentist. His name is _____.

2. Her name is Annie. She's a very good _____.

3. His name is Bill. He's a marvelous _____.

4. Her name is Sandy. _____ an excellent _____.

5. He's a _____ student. _____ name is Andy.


## 40  Argument Chant

Listen to your teacher read five questions. Then listen again and write the questions below. Check your answers in the Answer Key, page 99.

1. _____

2. _____

3. _____

4. _____

5. _____

Now work with a classmate and answer the questions above using the information from the chant. There are two possible answers for each question. Check your answers in the Answer Key, page 99.

1. _____

2. _____

3. _____

4. _____

5. _____

## 41 She's Nice. I Like Her.

Listen to your teacher read five sentences. Then listen again and write the sentences below. Check your answers in the Answer Key, page 99.

1. _____

2. _____

3. _____

4. _____

5. _____

## 42 I Don't Like Her. I Can't Help It.

Listen carefully as your teacher reads the sentences below. Then listen again as your teacher repeats them. Fill in the blanks with the correct words. Check your answers in the Answer Key, page 99.

1. I _____ like _____.

2. I _____ help _____.

3. I _____ stand _____.

4. She _____ irritates _____.

5. She _____ _____ crazy.

## 43 Everyone Spoke English at the Party Last Night

Answer the questions below. Use the information from the chant. Use complete sentences in your answers. Check your answers in the Answer Key, page 99.

1. Who spoke English at the party? _____

2. Did they speak very quickly? _____

3. Could you understand them? _____

4. Did you try to answer their questions? _____

5. Did you speak fast? _____


## 44 Fresh Fish

Answer the questions below. Use the information from the chant. Use complete sentences in your answers. Check your answers in the Answer Key, page 99.

1. What do they have for breakfast? _____

2. Is the fish fresh? _____

3. Who'll catch it? _____

4. Who'll cook it? _____

5. Who'll eat it? _____

## 45 Pete Eats Meat

Answer the questions below. Use the information from the chant. Use complete sentences in your answers. If you need more space, use a separate piece of paper. Check your answers in the Answer Key, page 99.

1. Who likes ham sandwiches? _____

2. Who likes clams? _____

3. Who eats vegetables every day? _____

4. Does Pete eat fish? _____

5. Does Marian eat meatloaf? _____

## 46 My PC

Write eight words that are associated with a personal computer. Use the information from the chant. Check your answers in the Answer Key, page 99.

_____

_____

_____

_____

_____

_____

_____

_____

## 47 Hospital Chant

Listen to your teacher read five questions. Then listen again and write the questions below. Check your answers in the Answer Key, page 99.

1. _____

2. _____

3. _____

4. _____

5. _____

Now work with a classmate and answer the questions above using the information from the chant. Use complete sentences in your answers. Check your answers in the Answer Key, page 99.

1. _____

2. _____

3. _____

4. _____

5. _____

## 48 I Hate Voice Mail

Fill in the blanks below with the correct words. Use the information from the chant. Check your answers in the Answer Key, page 99.

1. If you're calling from a touch-tone phone, _____ _____.

2. If you're calling from a _____ _____, press 8.

3. If you don't have a touch-tone phone, _____ _____.

4. Press _____ for the list of people to _____.

5. Press _____ if you want to. We don't care!

## 49 Weather Report

Listen to your teacher read five sentences. Then listen again and write the sentences below. Check your answers in the Answer Key, page 99.

1. _____

2. _____

3. _____

4. _____

5. _____

## 50 I Like the City

Listen carefully as your teacher reads the sentences below. Then listen again as your teacher repeats them. Fill in the blanks with the correct words. Check your answers in the Answer Key, page 99.

1. I like _____ city.

2. Look _____ the buildings _____ the sky.

3. I _____ the rhythm _____ the city _____.

4. I like _____ jazz. I _____ the _____.

5. My _____ city is _____ _____ night.

## 51 Harry Loves Mary

Complete the following sentences, using the pattern:
He loves her, but she doesn't love him.

1. She likes him, but _____.

2. We like them, but _____.

3. They like us, but _____.

4. He's crazy about her, but _____.

5. She's interested in him, but _____.


## 52 Catching Fish in Canada

Answer the questions below. Use the information from the chant. Use complete sentences in your answers. Check your answers in the Answer Key, page 100.

1. What are they building in Tokyo? _____

2. What are they drinking in London? _____

3. What are they selling in Maine? _____

4. What are they selling in Switzerland? _____

5. What are the kids reading in L.A.? _____

## 53 The Blue Jeans Blues

Listen to your teacher read five questions. Then listen again and write the questions below. Check your answers in the Answer Key, page 100.

1. _____

2. _____

3. _____

4. _____

5. _____

Now answer the questions above using the information from the chant. Use complete sentences in your answers. Check your answers in the Answer Key, page 100.

1. _____

2. _____

3. _____

4. _____

5. _____

## 54 Bobby's Back

Listen carefully as your teacher reads the sentences below. Then listen again as your teacher repeats them. Fill in the blanks with the correct words. Check your answers in the Answer Key, page 100.

1. Bobby's _____.

2. _____ _____ happy _____ Bobby's back.

3. _____ here.

4. _____ _____ happy _____ _____ back.

5. _____ happy _____ Bobby's back _____.

## 55 She Thinks About Him

Listen to your teacher read five questions. Then listen again and write the questions below. Check your answers in the Answer Key, page 100.

1. _____

2. _____

3. _____

4. _____

5. _____

Now answer the questions above using the information from the chant. Use complete sentences in your answers. Check your questions and answers in the Answer Key, page 100.

1. _____

2. _____

3. _____

4. _____

5. _____

# Part VII

## Answer Key

## 1 Sh! Sh! Baby's Sleeping!

1. The baby is sleeping.
2. Is the baby sleeping?
3. What did he say?
4. The babies aren't sleeping.
5. What did you say?

## 2 Do You Know Mary?

1. What is Mary's last name? Her last name is McDonald.
2. Who is Betty? Betty is Mary's older sister.
3. Who is Sue? Sue is Mary's younger sister.
4. What is the name of Mary's aunt? Her name is Esther.
5. What is the name of Mary's husband? His name is Bobby.

## 3 Tall Trees

1. The coast of California is a beautiful sight with the big, tall trees.
2. The trees in northern California are very, very tall.
3. Look at those tall trees!
4. Look at those redwood trees. They're huge.
5. What kind of tree is that? That's a California redwood tree.

## 4 Rain

1. It was raining hard.
2. It was falling on my shoes.
3. I got soaking wet.
4. The rain was warm.
5. It reminded me of home.

## 5 Major Decisions

Answers will vary.

## 6 Banker's Wife's Blues

**Questions**
1. Where does he live?
2. Where does he work?
3. When does he work?
4. Where does he study?
5. Where does he sleep?

**Answers**
1. He lives near the bank.
2. He works at the bank.
3. He works all day, and he works all night.
4. He studies at the bank.
5. He sleeps at the bank.

## 7 My Feet Hurt!

1. My feet hurt! Take off your shoes.
2. It's hot in here! Take off your sweater.
3. It's cold in here! Put on your sweater.
4. My hands are cold! Put on your gloves.

## 8 Departure and Return Home

1. Have a wonderful trip.
2. Don't forget to call me.
3. Gee, it's good to see you.
4. You look wonderful.
5. I'm so glad you're back.

## 9 Panic on Being Late

1. What time is it?
2. Hurry up! Hurry up!
3. We're going to be late.
4. I'm late, I'm late, I'm terribly late!
5. I don't have time to talk to you now.

## 10 Personal Questions

1. Where were you born?
2. Where were you last night?
3. How old are you?
4. How much rent do you pay?
5. Did you stay out late?
6–10. Questions will vary.

## 11 Mama Knows Best

1. You shouldn't do it that way.
2. You ought to do it this way.
3. He shouldn't go with them.
4. She ought to take the bus.
5. You ought to cut your hair.
6–10. Answers will vary.

## 12 On the Rocks

1. You never listen to me.
2. He never talks to me.
3. He just sits around and watches TV.
4. She never listens to me.
5. What did you say?

## 13 Taking Credit

1. Whose book is this?
2. Whose work is this?
3. Whose bookbag is this?
4. Whose pen is that?
5. Whose cup is that?
6–10. Answers will vary.

Answer Key

## 14 It's Got to Be Somewhere

1. Where is it?
2. I can't find it.
3. It's got to be here.
4. It has to be here.
5. Try to remember.

## 15 Twelve Cans of Tuna Fish Rag

1. What does she eat? She eats fish./She eats twelve cans of (tuna) fish.
2. What kind of fish does she eat? She eats tuna fish.
3. How many cans of tuna does she eat? She eats twelve cans./She eats twelve cans of tuna fish.
4. How often does she eat those twelve cans? She eats twelve cans of tuna every night.
5. Is that a lot of fish? It sure is!/Yes, it is.

## 16 I Gave It Away

### Questions
1. What did you say?
2. Why did you give it away?
3. Why didn't you sell it?
4. Why didn't you give it to me?
5. Why didn't you give it to them?

### Answers
1. I said, "I gave it away."
2. Because I wanted to.
3. I didn't want to.
4. I didn't want to.
5. I didn't want to.

## 17 Selfish

1. This is mine! That's yours!
2. Don't touch mine! Get your own!
3. What are you doing with that?
4. What's his is his.
5. What's theirs is theirs.

## 18 Easy Solutions

### Complaints
1. I'm hungry.
2. I'm angry.
3. I'm sleepy.
4. It's hot in here.
5. I have a toothache.

### Solutions
1. Have a sandwich.
2. Calm down.
3. Take a nap.
4. Open a window.
5. Go to the dentist.

## 19 Wake Up! Wake Up!

1. What time is it?
2. I don't want to get up.
3. You have to get up.
4. You must get up.
5. You've got to get up.

## 20 You're Just Like Your Mother

### Sentences
1. Stop arguing with me.
2. Yes, you are.
3. You're just like your mother.
4. She loves to argue.
5. She does, too!

### Negative Statements
1. I'm not arguing with you.
2. No, I'm not.
3. I am not.
4. No, she doesn't!
5. She does not.

## 21 He Speaks English

1. He speaks English.
2. So does she.
3. She was born in Paris.
4. He grew up in New York.
5. So did she.

## 22 God Save the TOEFL Test

1. Did you take the TOEFL test? Yes, I did.
2. Was the test hard? Yes, it was.
3. Did you get a stomachache? Yes, I did.
4. Did your eyes fill up with tears? Yes, they did.
5. What did your teacher promise you? She promised that I'd speak (English) fluently.
6–7. Answers will vary.

## 23 Henry Wants to Go to Harvard

### Questions
1. What does Henry want?
2. Where does he want to graduate from?
3. Does he want to learn to ski?
4. Does he have a cell phone?
5. Does he have a VCR?

### Answers
1. He wants an MBA.
2. He wants to graduate from Harvard or from Yale.
3. Yes, he does.
4. Yes, he does.
5. Yes, he does.

## 24 Love Song
1. Yes, she does.
2. Yes, he is.
3. Yes, he does.
4. Yes, they are.
5. Yes, he will (if he has to).

## 25 I Told Him and He Told Her
1. I told him.
2. He told her.
3. She told me.
4. They told us.
5. We told her.

## 26 The Telephone Rang, But I Didn't Answer It
1. She gave him a sweater, but he didn't wear it.
2. He gave her a book, but she didn't read it.
3. They gave us a car, but we didn't drive it.
4. We gave them a cake, but they didn't eat it.
5. I gave him a bike, but he didn't ride it.

## 27 Cucamonga, California
**Questions**
1. Where was he born?
2. When was he born?
3. Where did he grow up?
4. Where is Cucamonga?
5. How long did he live in Cucamonga?

**Answers**
1. He was born in Cucamonga.
2. He was born on a bright September day.
3. He grew up in Cucamonga.
4. It's in California, U.S.A.
5. He lived in Cucamonga for ninety years.

## 28 The Chocolate Cake Song
**Questions**
1. What kind of cake did he eat?
2. Did he eat a pizza pie?
3. What happened to him?
4. What did he drink?
5. Did he need a pharmacy?

**Answers**
1. He ate a chocolate cake.
2. Yes, he did.
3. He got a stomachache.
4. He drank some herbal tea.
5. Yes, he did.

## 29 He Speaks English
Answers will vary.

## 30 The Red Umbrella
1. What did you buy? I bought a red umbrella.
2. Where did you leave your red umbrella? I left it on the train.
3. Did you lose your red umbrella? Yes, I did.
4. Where did you find an old umbrella? I found it on the sidewalk, near the train.
5. Do you think it's going to rain today? Yes, I do./I'm sure it's going to rain.

## 31 Pizza Chant
Answers will vary.

## 32 Are You Free for Lunch?
1. Are you free for lunch?
2. It'll have to be early.
3. Let's meet at noon.
4. Can you take a break?
5. Not right now. I've got a deadline to make.

## 33 The Hamburger Chant
Answers will vary.

## 34 I Wonder What Time It Is
1. I wonder what time it is.
2. I hope it's not late.
3. Oh, good! It's only eight.
4. Oh, no! It's nine o'clock.
5. I'm late!

## 35 My Computer's Down
1. What's the matter?
2. What's the problem?
3. My computer's down.
4. Things are bad and getting worse.
5. What'll I do?

## 36 The Answering Machine Blues
1. Sorry, we're out.
2. Leave your name and number.
3. Your call is important.
4. We'll call you right back.
5. We'll get right back just as soon as we can.

## 37 Fast Food
**Questions**
1. What are you going to have?
2. What kind of bread?
3. What kind of cheese?
4. Anything to drink?
5. Large or small?

**Answers**
1. I'd like a grilled cheese sandwich.
2. Rye bread.
3. American cheese.
4. Coffee, please.
5. Large, please.

## 38 E-mail Boogie
1. I love E-mail.
2. I do, too.
3. So will you.
4. They get E-mail every day.
5. So do they.

## 39 He's a Wonderful Dentist
1. He's a wonderful dentist. His name is Danny.
2. Her name is Annie. She's a very good patient.
3. His name is Bill. He's a marvelous singer.
4. Her name is Sandy. She's an excellent teacher.
5. He's a brilliant student. His name is Andy.

## 40 Argument Chant
**Questions**
1. Is he a good student?
2. Does he study every day?
3. Does he write very well?
4. Does he speak very well?
5. Is he usually on time?

**Answers**
1. Yes, he is./No, he isn't.
2. Yes, he does./No, he doesn't.
3. Yes, he does./No, he doesn't.
4. Yes, he does./No, he doesn't.
5. Yes, he is./No, he isn't.

## 41 She's Nice. I Like Her.
1. She's nice. I like her.
2. I really like her very much.
3. He's nice.
4. He's really very nice.
5. I really like them very much.

## 42 I Don't Like Her. I Can't Help It.
1. I don't like her.
2. I can't help it.
3. I can't stand her.
4. She really irritates me.
5. She drives me crazy.

## 43 Everyone Spoke English at the Party Last Night
1. Who spoke English at the party? Everyone spoke English at the party./Everyone did.
2. Did they speak very quickly? Yes, they did.
3. Could you understand them? No, I couldn't.
4. Did you try to answer their questions? Yes, I did.
5. Did you speak fast? No, I didn't.

## 44 Fresh Fish
1. What do they have for breakfast? They have fresh fish.
2. Is the fish fresh? Yes, it is.
3. Who'll catch it? She will.
4. Who'll cook it? He will.
5. Who'll eat it? We will.

## 45 Pete Eats Meat
1. Who likes ham sandwiches? Pete does./Pete likes ham sandwiches.
2. Who likes clams? Trish does./Trish loves clams.
3. Who eats vegetables every day? Marian does./Marian eats vegetables every day.
4. Does Pete like fish? No, he doesn't (like fish).
5. Does Marian eat meatloaf? No, she doesn't (eat meatloaf).

## 46 My PC
cursor
keyboard
monitor
mouse
diskette
disk drive
CD
power supply

## 47 Hospital Chant
**Questions**
1. Who's on crutches?
2. Who's in a cast?
3. Who's in a wheelchair?
4. Who's on a stretcher?
5. Who has the flu?

**Answers**
1. Kenny's on crutches.
2. Cathy's in a cast.
3. Willie's in a wheelchair.
4. Sally's on a stretcher.
5. Frankie has the flu.

## 48 I Hate Voice Mail

1. If you're calling from a touch-tone phone, press 1.
2. If you're calling from a mobile phone, press 8.
3. If you don't have a touch-tone phone, say "Two."
4. Press 4 for the list of people to call.
5. Press 7 if you want to. We don't care!

## 49 Weather Report

1. Will it rain today, or will it snow?
2. Don't listen to the forecasters. They don't know.
3. The weatherman says we won't have rain.
4. He promised us sunshine, and what did we get?
5. We got very, very wet.

## 50 I Like the City

1. I like the city.
2. Look at the buildings touching the sky.
3. I like the rhythm on the city street.
4. I like the jazz. I like the park.
5. My favorite city is up all night.

## 51 Harry Loves Mary

1. She likes him, but he doesn't like her.
2. We like them, but they don't like us.
3. They like us, but we don't like them.
4. He's crazy about her, but she isn't crazy about him.
5. She's interested in him, but he isn't interested in her.

## 52 Catching Fish in Canada

1. What are they building in Tokyo? They're building cars.
2. What are they drinking in London? They're drinking tea.
3. What are they selling in Maine? They're selling fish.
4. What are they selling in Switzerland? They're selling books.
5. What are the kids reading in L.A.? They're reading comic books.

## 53 The Blue Jeans Blues

**Questions**

1. Does she wear blue jeans?
2. Does she wear jeans in the winter?
3. Does she wear jeans in the summer?
4. What does she wear with her blue jeans?
5. Does she look good?

**Answers**

1. Yes, she does.
2. Yes, she does.
3. Yes, she does.
4. She wears a T-shirt with her blue jeans.
5. Yes, she does.

## 54 Bobby's Back

1. Bobby's back.
2. I'm so happy that Bobby's back.
3. Bobby's here.
4. You're so happy that Bobby's back.
5. Everybody's happy that Bobby's back again.

## 55 She Thinks About Him

**Questions**

1. Who does she think about?
2. Who does she talk about?
3. Who does she dream about?
4. When does she dream about him?
5. Does she think about him all the time?

**Answers**

1. She thinks about him.
2. She talks about him.
3. She dreams about him.
4. She dreams about him all the time.
5. Yes, she does.

Answer Key

# Index to Chants and Songs